I FOUGHT THE LAW

Ann Ming's Fight for Justice and the Case That Changed Britain.

John S. Ruf

All rights reserved. No part of this publication may be reproduced, distributed, or transmitted in any form or by any means, including photocopying, recording, or other electronic or mechanical methods, without the prior written permission of the publisher, except in the case of brief quotations embodied in critical reviews and certain other noncommercial uses permitted by copyright law.

Copyright © John S. Ruf. 2025.

TABLE OF CONTENTS

INTRODUCTION

CHAPTER 1: A NORMAL LIFE IN BILLINGHAM
   Julie Hogg's World
   A Close-Knit Family

CHAPTER 2: THE DISAPPEARANCE
   The Last Night Seen
   A Mother's Unease

CHAPTER 3: THE SEARCH FOR JULIE
   Community in Fear
   Clues That Went Nowhere

CHAPTER 4: THE HEARTBREAKING DISCOVERY
   Behind the Bath Panel
   Grief Beyond Words

CHAPTER 5: FIRST STEPS TOWARD JUSTICE
   Forensic Hopes
   Trial One: Doubt in the Jury Box

CHAPTER 6: THE PAIN OF ACQUITTAL
   Trial Two: Another Collapse
   The Double Jeopardy Shield

CHAPTER 7: LIVING UNDER THE SHADOW
   Dunlop Walks Free

The Weight on Ann's Family

CHAPTER 8: A KILLER CONFESSES
  The Prison Admission
  Perjury and Frustration

CHAPTER 9: THE CAMPAIGN OF A LIFETIME
  Letters, Meetings, and Parliament
  Building Public Support

CHAPTER 10: OVERTURNING AN ANCIENT LAW
  The Criminal Justice Act 2003
  How Double Jeopardy Fell

CHAPTER 11: JUSTICE AT THE OLD BAILEY
  Dunlop Retrial and Conviction
  A Mother's Victory After 17 Years

CHAPTER 12: LEGACY AND REFLECTION
  Ann Ming's Recognition and MBE
  How Her Fight Changed Britain

CONCLUSION

INTRODUCTION

On a cold November night in 1989, a young mother vanished without a trace from her quiet home in Billingham, County Durham. Twenty-two-year-old Julie Hogg was loved by her family, devoted to her little boy, and known by her neighbors as a kind soul with her whole future ahead of her. When she failed to return home, her mother, Ann Ming, knew in her bones that something was terribly wrong. What began as a missing person's case would soon unravel into one of the most shocking and frustrating legal battles in modern British history.

Julie's killer, Billy Dunlop, was caught, tried, and despite damning forensic evidence twice acquitted. The centuries-old double jeopardy law meant that no matter what new proof came to light, he could never be tried again. For Ann Ming, that was not justice. It was a loophole that mocked her daughter's memory and gave a murderer freedom. As Dunlop bragged in pubs about "getting away with the perfect crime," Ann refused to give in to despair. Instead, she began an unrelenting fight that would span more than a decade, take her into the halls of Parliament, and force Britain to change an 800-year-old law.

This is not just the story of a brutal crime. It is the story of a mother's courage, a legal system pushed to its limits, and a battle that proved one person's determination can reshape the course of history. *I Fought the Law: Ann Ming's Fight for Justice and the Case That Changed Britain* takes you inside the heartbreak, the trials, the failures, and finally, the triumph that made Ann Ming's campaign one of the most extraordinary quests for justice the country has ever known.

CHAPTER 1: A NORMAL LIFE IN BILLINGHAM

Julie Hogg's World

Julie Hogg was just twenty-two years old in the autumn of 1989, and to those who knew her best, she seemed to radiate a quiet strength and kindness that left a mark on everyone she encountered. Born and raised in Billingham, a modest town in County Durham, Julie lived in the sort of community where families had deep roots and neighbors often felt more like extended family. She grew up in a household that valued loyalty, hard work, and love, and those values shaped the woman she became. Friends remembered her as cheerful, compassionate, and dependable, the kind of person who could brighten a dull day with her laughter. Her presence filled a room without demanding attention, a rare quality that made people naturally gravitate toward her.

Life had not always been easy for Julie, but she met challenges with determination. She was the mother of a little boy, Kevin, and caring for him was at the center of her world. For a young woman in her early twenties, raising a child could have been overwhelming, but Julie embraced motherhood with pride and devotion. Those closest to her often said that her face lit up whenever she spoke of Kevin, her voice softening as she described his milestones and daily adventures. He was not just her son; he was her anchor and her greatest joy. Everything she worked for — every job she held, every plan she made — was tied to giving him the stability and love she felt he deserved.

Julie's independence was another defining trait. She worked hard to support herself and her child, balancing responsibilities that might have weighed heavily on someone else her age. Her determination showed in the way she carried herself, refusing to let circumstances diminish her spirit. Friends admired her resilience, often remarking on how she managed to juggle motherhood and work without losing her sense of humor. She was not wealthy, nor did she aspire to live a glamorous life, but she had dreams — dreams of building a secure future for Kevin, of creating a home filled with love, laughter, and stability. Those dreams, though modest to some, were profound to her, and they reflected her values and her sense of responsibility.

At the center of Julie's life was her mother, Ann Ming, who was both her confidante and her rock. The bond between mother and daughter was unshakable. Ann often described Julie as not just her child, but her closest friend. They shared secrets, celebrated small victories together, and leaned on each other in times of uncertainty. Ann admired her daughter's courage and grit, while Julie cherished her mother's constant support and unconditional love. That closeness was obvious to those who observed them; their connection was not just one of family ties but of deep friendship, and it became a source of strength for both women.

Julie's life may have seemed ordinary to outsiders, but within her small circle, it was rich with meaning and filled with promise. She was a devoted mother, a beloved daughter, and a loyal friend. She had dreams for the future, and she carried them with quiet determination. No one could have anticipated how brutally that life would be cut short, or how her death would expose the flaws in a centuries-old legal system. What began as the story of a missing young woman would unravel into a tragedy that shook her family to its core — and ultimately sparked a fight that changed the course of British justice forever.

A Close-Knit Family

The Ming and Hogg families were the kind that held tightly to one another, weathering life's ups and downs together. They lived in a community where family was the center of everything, and for Ann Ming, her children were her greatest treasure. Julie was her only daughter, and their bond went far beyond the usual ties of parent and child. Ann often saw herself reflected in Julie's determination and warmth, and the closeness between them was a source of strength for both women. Julie leaned on her mother for guidance and support, while Ann cherished every moment of being not only a parent but a friend to her daughter. The affection between them was genuine, visible in the way they spoke, the comfort they found in each other's company, and the shared responsibility they felt in raising Kevin, Julie's young son.

Kevin's arrival had deepened the family's sense of unity. Though Julie and her husband's relationship was fragile and on the verge of ending, the little boy was never without love. Ann stepped in as a grandmother with the same devotion she had shown as a mother, creating a strong safety net around Julie and Kevin. To her, family was not just about blood ties but about presence — being there in times of need, celebrating milestones together, and never letting anyone feel alone. For Kevin, this meant a childhood surrounded by people who adored him, people who worked hard to ensure he felt secure despite the changes happening in his parents' relationship.

This closeness wasn't limited to just Julie, Kevin, and Ann. The wider family, including siblings, cousins, and extended relatives, often played a role in each other's lives. In a town like Billingham, families lived just streets apart, popping in on one another unannounced, sharing meals, and leaning on each other for support. Holidays and birthdays were filled with laughter, home-cooked food, and the kind of chaos only big families can bring. That environment, built on loyalty and trust, helped shape Julie's values and gave her a foundation of love she wanted to pass on to her son. The idea of family wasn't abstract; it was lived daily in countless small acts of kindness and care.

Julie herself was central to maintaining that bond. Though she was young, she carried herself with a sense of responsibility toward those around her, always looking out for friends and family alike. Her natural instinct was to nurture, to care, and to bring people together. She often leaned on her mother for help, but she also gave back in the ways she could — offering companionship, laughter, and loyalty. Her presence was reassuring, and the people in her life drew comfort from knowing she was there. In many ways, Julie's home became an extension of her mother's, a place where warmth and love were guaranteed.

For Ann, the idea of family meant sacrifice as much as joy. She worked hard to ensure her children and grandchild had everything they needed, even when it demanded her time and energy. Yet she never viewed this as a burden; it was her purpose, and she embraced it wholeheartedly. That sense of devotion created a protective shield around her family, but it also left her vulnerable to unimaginable heartbreak. When Julie disappeared, it was not only the loss of a daughter but the unraveling of a family's entire foundation. The closeness that had once been their greatest strength was tested in the cruelest way imaginable, forcing Ann to summon courage she didn't know she possessed.

CHAPTER 2: THE DISAPPEARANCE

The Last Night Seen

On the evening of 16 November 1989, Julie Hogg's life seemed to move along as ordinarily as any other night. The air was cold in Billingham, the kind of sharp November chill that settled into the streets and kept most people indoors. For Julie, the day had been filled with her usual mix of responsibilities — caring for her son, running errands, and keeping her small world in order. That night, she was expected to return home, unwind, and prepare for another day of balancing motherhood and work. Nothing about those final hours suggested the tragedy that was about to unfold.

As the evening wore on, Julie crossed paths with William "Billy" Dunlop, a man from her neighborhood who had a reputation for trouble. Dunlop had spent the night drinking heavily and causing disturbances at Billingham Rugby Club, where his aggression had already flared during arguments. He left the club with a bruised face and a short temper, a man whose judgment was clouded by alcohol and frustration. On his way home, he decided to stop at Julie's house. He knew her from the community and, emboldened by drink and entitlement, arrived at her door expecting companionship, perhaps even intimacy.

Julie, however, wanted nothing to do with his advances. She was not interested in Dunlop that night or any night. Accounts suggest she made a lighthearted remark about his swollen eye, but instead of brushing it off, Dunlop's pride was wounded. His anger rose quickly, spiraling into violence. In a sudden and uncontrollable fit of rage, he strangled Julie in her own home. The attack was brutal and senseless, robbing her of her life in a matter of moments. Julie's warmth, her laughter, and her dreams for her little boy ended that night, extinguished by an act of cruelty she never saw coming.

In a desperate attempt to conceal what he had done, Dunlop hid Julie's body. He wrapped her in a blanket and forced her beneath the bath panel in her bathroom, crudely disguising the evidence of his crime. To him, it may have seemed like a quick solution, but it was the beginning of a long nightmare for her family. He left her there, trapped in silence, while outside the world carried on unaware. For Ann Ming and those who loved Julie, her sudden disappearance would soon become an agonizing mystery.

That night was the last time anyone outside her home saw Julie alive. Neighbors, friends, and family assumed she would carry on with her life as always, caring for her son and spending time with her mother. Instead, she vanished without explanation, leaving behind unanswered questions and a mother's instinctive fear that something was terribly wrong. What unfolded from that night forward was not only a murder investigation, but a battle against indifference, missteps, and a legal system ill-equipped to deliver justice. For Ann, the clock stopped that November evening, though she could not yet know just how much strength the next thirteen years would demand of her.

A Mother's Unease

When Julie failed to return home or make contact, Ann Ming felt an immediate shift in her heart. To some, a young woman missing for a day might have seemed explainable — perhaps she had stayed with a friend, perhaps she needed time alone, perhaps the busyness of life had pulled her away temporarily. But Ann knew her daughter. Julie was a devoted mother whose little boy was always her first thought. She would never leave him without explanation. That silence, that absence, spoke louder to Ann than any words ever could. Something was wrong, and Ann felt it in her bones.

At first, the police and even some neighbors treated Julie's disappearance as though it might have been voluntary. Suggestions surfaced that she had run off, that she might be trying to start a new life. These assumptions, often thrown casually in Ann's direction, only deepened her frustration. She knew her daughter's character, her routines, and her devotion to her family. Julie was not the type to vanish without telling anyone. The idea that she had simply "walked away" was both insulting and untrue. Ann's unease hardened into conviction — she was certain her daughter had met with harm.

Ann's days quickly turned into a restless cycle of phone calls, knocking on doors, and checking with anyone who might have seen Julie last. She walked the streets of Billingham searching for clues, retracing steps, asking questions, trying desperately to piece together a trail that the police seemed too slow to follow. Nights brought no rest. She would sit awake, replaying conversations, wondering if she had missed a warning sign, questioning whether there was something more she could do to bring Julie home. That gnawing uncertainty consumed her, pushing her into action even as exhaustion wore her down.

The most haunting part of Ann's unease was the gnawing intuition that Julie was not just missing but gone forever. A mother's instinct rarely falters, and Ann could not shake the image of her daughter in danger, harmed by someone who had taken her away from them. She tried to push those thoughts aside, to cling to the hope of finding Julie alive, but every hour that passed without word made hope harder to hold onto. In its place grew an unshakable determination: if the police would not find answers, she would demand them until someone did.

Ann's unease was more than worry. It was the beginning of a thirteen-year fight for truth and justice. It was the spark that fueled her relentless pursuit of answers, even as others dismissed her concerns. What began as a mother's intuition became the foundation of a campaign that would not only uncover Julie's fate but eventually change the course of British law. Long before the courts or Parliament knew her name, Ann Ming was already standing firm in her belief — a daughter's disappearance is never "just another case" when a mother knows something is terribly wrong.

CHAPTER 3: THE SEARCH FOR JULIE

Community in Fear

As the days stretched into weeks with no sign of Julie, the unease that gripped her family began to spread across Billingham. What had once been a close, ordinary town where neighbors trusted one another now carried an air of suspicion and dread. People who once left their doors unlocked began double-checking bolts at night. Parents warned their children not to walk alone, and small, everyday routines suddenly seemed tinged with danger. Julie's disappearance was not just the loss of a daughter, friend, and mother — it was a rupture in the community's sense of safety.

The police presence, though visible at times, did little to settle fears. Patrol cars circled, officers asked questions, and flyers with Julie's face appeared in shop windows, but no answers came. Rumors filled the silence where truth should have been. Some speculated about strangers passing through town, others whispered that someone local was responsible. The lack of progress in the investigation made people restless, and every unknown face or odd sound in the night seemed magnified by fear. Julie's story became a cautionary tale repeated in hushed voices, a grim reminder that danger could strike even in familiar places.

Friends of Julie, especially young women, began to alter their lives in ways they never had before. They traveled in pairs, arranged check-in calls, and made sure someone always knew where they were going. Men in the community, too, felt the shadow of suspicion. Those who had crossed paths with Julie around the time she vanished found themselves questioned, their names passed around in conversations they couldn't control. A subtle but sharp divide grew: trust was eroding, and fear was breeding suspicion among people who had once been neighbors and friends.

For Ann Ming, the sight of her community living in fear only deepened her anguish. Each unanswered question, each child warned to stay close, underscored the truth she already felt Julie's disappearance was not a mistake or a whim. Someone had done this, and until that person was found, everyone was at risk. Ann carried not only her grief but the weight of knowing her daughter's fate had changed the lives of so many others around her. It wasn't just her family in mourning; it was an entire town on edge.

The community's fear became a kind of collective wound, one that would not heal until Julie's story was fully told and justice delivered. Streets once filled with laughter and chatter seemed quieter, weighed down by the absence of answers. Neighbors, once quick to greet each other, now cast cautious glances, wondering who might know more than they were saying. In this tense atmosphere, the need for truth was no longer just Ann's — it was everyone's. And yet, even with the weight of a town behind her, Ann often felt she was the only one truly pushing for the fight that lay ahead.

Clues That Went Nowhere

In the first weeks of Julie's disappearance, police followed up on leads that seemed promising but ultimately led to disappointment. A sighting here, a rumor there — each new piece of information offered a flicker of hope that quickly burned out. Some claimed to have seen Julie walking late at night; others insisted she had been spotted in nearby towns. Officers chased these reports, questioning strangers, pulling records, and checking bus stations, but every lead dissolved into nothing. Each dead end was more than a setback;

it was a cruel cycle of lifted spirits and crushing letdowns for Ann and her family.

One of the greatest frustrations for Ann was how quickly the investigation seemed to stall. Detectives often treated tips as if they were little more than nuisances, brushing them aside when they didn't immediately fit a neat explanation. There was talk that Julie may have left willingly, starting anew somewhere far away. To Ann, these theories were not only insulting but dangerous. They took the focus off what she knew to be true: her daughter had been taken from her, and every wasted moment allowed whoever was responsible to slip further from reach.

The community, eager to help, often supplied information that turned out to be nothing more than gossip. People speculated about Julie's personal life, her friendships, even her habits, trying to piece together answers in the absence of facts. Each time Ann heard such talk, it cut deeply. She knew Julie as more than the whispers painted her, and she feared the noise distracted investigators from looking in the right places. In many ways, the rumors became another form of injustice, clouding the search for the real truth.

Police searches of local buildings, alleyways, and fields turned up little evidence. Homes were checked, waterways scanned, and tips reviewed, but nothing materialized. The absence of physical clues made the case all the more frustrating. It was as though Julie had vanished into thin air, leaving behind no trace that could point to what happened. For Ann, the silence of these searches was unbearable — each time officers emerged empty-handed, it felt like another dismissal of her certainty that her daughter was in danger.

"Clues that went nowhere" became the cruel refrain of the investigation's early days. With each false lead, the distance between Julie's disappearance and the truth seemed to widen. Ann's trust in the system began to waver, replaced by a hardening resolve that she could not depend solely on the authorities to deliver answers. The police may have been stuck chasing shadows, but Ann was already beginning to prepare herself for the long battle ahead — a battle that would require her to fight harder, shout louder, and refuse to let her daughter's story be lost in a maze of dead ends.

CHAPTER 4: THE HEARTBREAKING DISCOVERY

Behind the Bath Panel

The breakthrough came not in some sweeping police operation, but in the most ordinary of places — Julie's own home. For weeks, officers and volunteers had searched fields, rivers, abandoned buildings, and backstreets, but the answer had been lying just a few feet away from where Julie should have felt safest. It was only when a persistent search of her home was carried out again that someone thought to look more closely at the bathroom. There, hidden behind the bath panel, lay the heartbreaking truth: Julie's body, concealed in the very house she had lived in.

The discovery was a moment of horror that shook everyone involved. For Ann Ming, it was confirmation of her worst fears, the moment her mother's instinct was proven right in the cruelest way possible. Julie had not walked away. She had not started a new life. She had been silenced, hidden, and left in a place that should have been sanctuary. The brutality of the concealment added another layer of pain — not only had Julie been killed, but she had been denied dignity in death, tucked away as though her life meant nothing.

For the police, the discovery was both a relief and a humiliation. Relief because they had finally found Julie, ending weeks of speculation and fear. Humiliation because they had missed it, not once but several times. The fact that Julie's body had lain undiscovered in her own home for so long raised serious questions about the quality of the investigation. How could officers have overlooked something so critical? How many times had Ann been told to trust that they were doing all they could, only for this to come to light? The oversight deepened Ann's mistrust, hardening her resolve to keep pushing for accountability.

The community, too, was shaken to its core. To know that Julie had been so close all along was devastating, and it reignited fears that the killer was among them — perhaps someone they had spoken to, passed in the street, or even shared a pint with at the local pub. The sense of betrayal, of innocence lost, was profound. This was no longer just a missing persons case; it was a murder, and one that proved evil could lurk far closer than anyone wanted to believe.

For Ann, the moment of discovery was the beginning of her second fight. Finding Julie brought closure in one sense — she no longer had to wonder where her daughter was. But it also ignited a deeper, more painful journey: the pursuit of justice. Whoever had taken Julie's life had stolen not only a daughter, mother, and friend but also a future. Behind the bath panel, Ann found the truth she had long feared. Now she would dedicate herself to making sure the world knew it too, and that justice would not be denied.

Grief Beyond Words

The moment Julie's body was discovered shattered the fragile hope Ann Ming had clung to. Though her instincts had long whispered the truth, nothing could prepare her for the brutal confirmation. The sight of her daughter, hidden and discarded like a secret, was seared into her memory. Ann's grief was raw, overwhelming, and unrelenting — a pain that defied expression. There are no words strong enough to capture what it means to lose a child in such a violent and senseless way. It was not only the end of Julie's life but also the end of a future filled with laughter, milestones, and family memories that would now never be made.

In the days following the discovery, Ann moved through a fog of sorrow, each breath heavy with loss. The sound of her grandson's voice, the familiarity of Julie's belongings, even the silence of her home seemed unbearable reminders of what had been taken. Grief became both a constant weight and an ever-shifting storm, one moment numbing, the next erupting with rage, disbelief, and unbearable sorrow. She was forced to do what no mother should ever have to — bury her child, and face the unimaginable reality of life without her.

The community mourned alongside Ann. Vigils were held, flowers left at Julie's door, and messages of sympathy poured in. Yet for Ann, those gestures, though kind, could not touch the depth of her despair. People told her she was strong, but she did not feel strong; she felt broken, emptied, and furious at the cruelty of the world. The public nature of Julie's death, whispered about in pubs and splashed across headlines, only deepened the wound. Ann's private grief was now a spectacle, her family's pain exposed for all to see.

What compounded the agony was the sense that Julie's dignity had been stolen twice — first in her murder, and again in the careless investigation that had failed to find her sooner. Ann could not stop replaying the weeks of unanswered questions, the assurances from police that nothing was wrong, and the gut feeling she had been forced to suppress. If someone had only listened, perhaps Julie's body would have been found earlier, sparing her family the additional trauma of those long months of uncertainty. That failure haunted Ann, fueling a grief that was inseparable from anger.

Still, beneath the sorrow, there was something else — a flicker of determination. Ann's grief, though beyond words, carried within it a seed of resolve. She would not let Julie's life, or her death, be forgotten. She would not let the man responsible escape justice, nor the system's failures go unchallenged. Grief had stripped her to the core, but it had also revealed a strength she did not yet understand. Julie had been stolen from her, but Ann was determined that her daughter's story would not end in silence.

CHAPTER 5: FIRST STEPS TOWARD JUSTICE

Forensic Hopes

In the aftermath of Julie's discovery, investigators turned to forensic science, clinging to the hope that evidence would speak where witnesses could not. The house was combed for clues, every surface inspected, every object bagged and labeled. Fibers, fingerprints, and traces of blood were examined with the meticulous care that the initial investigation had sorely lacked. Forensic specialists worked to reconstruct Julie's final hours, searching for anything that might tie her killer directly to the crime. Ann Ming, though devastated, found a glimmer of comfort in believing that science, precise and impartial, might finally deliver the truth the police had failed to uncover on their own.

At that time, however, forensic technology was far from the sophisticated science it would later become. DNA testing was in its early stages, limited in scope and reliability. Samples that today could be analyzed with remarkable precision often produced inconclusive or weak results. Detectives tried to draw what they could from the evidence — the positioning of the body, the fibers on Julie's clothing, the fingerprints in the home — but many findings were circumstantial. They hinted at a suspect, but they did not yet create an airtight case. It was a frustrating reminder of how the system could lag behind the cruelty of crime.

The results pointed toward one man: Billy Dunlop, Julie's neighbor and a figure already clouded in suspicion. Forensic traces, though not definitive, connected him to the scene in troubling ways. Combined with his history of violence and his proximity to Julie's life, the picture grew clearer. Still, the investigators knew that to convince a jury, the evidence had to be stronger. Circumstantial connections, no matter how convincing, could be torn apart in court. The weight of proof was heavy, and the fear that a killer could walk free because of scientific limits hung over the case.

Ann, following the updates closely, placed her faith in the forensic process. She believed that the lab results would finally bring justice for Julie, finally hold the man she suspected accountable. Each time she heard of another test being run, she waited anxiously for the call that would confirm what she already knew in her heart. But the waiting was agonizing. Weeks turned into months, and the promises of answers seemed endlessly delayed. For a grieving mother, the slow grind of science was unbearable, especially when justice felt so close, yet so far.

In the end, forensics alone could not carry the case across the finish line. The science of the time provided important pieces of the puzzle but lacked the conclusive power to shut the door on doubt. It was a bitter truth: Julie's case might depend not just on evidence, but on persistence, pressure, and the willingness to fight against a system too easily swayed by loopholes and technicalities. For Ann Ming, those hopes rooted in forensics would become just one part of a much longer and harder journey — a journey that would eventually demand more than science could give.

Trial One: Doubt in the Jury Box

The courtroom was charged with anticipation when Billy Dunlop finally stood trial for the murder of Julie Hogg. For Ann Ming and her family, it was a moment they had long waited for — a chance to see the man they believed had taken Julie's life face justice. The evidence was laid out: his violent history, the inconsistencies in his statements, and the forensic traces that pointed his way. On the surface, it seemed like the path to a conviction was clear. Yet Ann quickly learned that trials are not battles of truth alone; they are contests of persuasion, strategy, and doubt.

From the very beginning, Dunlop's defense seized on the weaknesses in the prosecution's case. They painted the forensic evidence as circumstantial, emphasizing that the science could not place him at the exact moment of Julie's death. They attacked the credibility of witnesses, casting shadows on their memories and motives. Their arguments were not about proving his innocence outright but about planting enough uncertainty in the jurors' minds to prevent a unanimous guilty verdict. In the delicate balance of justice, doubt became their most powerful weapon.

Ann sat through the proceedings with a mix of fury and disbelief. She could not reconcile the picture the defense painted with the man she knew to be guilty. She watched as her daughter's life was reduced to timelines, testimonies, and exhibits, each detail dissected by strangers. To her, the truth was plain: Julie had been murdered by Dunlop. But to the jury, the case was a puzzle with missing pieces, and the law required certainty. That gap between a mother's certainty and a jury's doubt left Ann feeling powerless, her voice stifled in the very arena meant to deliver justice.

When the jury retired to deliberate, hope still flickered. Ann prayed they would see through the defense's tactics and recognize the truth in the evidence. But the hours dragged on, and whispers of division reached the gallery. Finally, the verdict came: not guilty. The words crashed over Ann like a tidal wave. Her heart sank as Dunlop, smirking with relief, walked out of court a free man. It was not just the failure of the system she felt in that moment, but a betrayal — a reminder that the truth alone was not enough to secure justice.

For Ann and her family, the acquittal was devastating. They left the courtroom broken, angry, and bewildered by how a man they believed guilty could so easily evade punishment. Worse still, they were told that the principle of "double jeopardy" meant Dunlop could never be tried again for Julie's murder, no matter what evidence might come to light in the future. That law, ancient and unyielding, slammed the door on their hopes for justice. Ann's fight was not over, but in that moment, it seemed the world had abandoned her.

CHAPTER 6: THE PAIN OF ACQUITTAL

Trial Two: Another Collapse

Despite the devastating outcome of the first trial, prosecutors were determined to try again when additional evidence emerged. For Ann Ming, it felt like a second chance — a rare opportunity to correct what had gone wrong the first time. She walked into the courtroom with renewed hope, praying that the weight of the evidence would finally expose Billy Dunlop for who he was. The family braced themselves for another round of painful testimony, steeling themselves to hear Julie's name spoken in the past tense once again. This time, they told themselves, the system would not fail.

But almost from the start, cracks began to show. The evidence, while compelling, was still not airtight by legal standards. Witnesses repeated their accounts, yet the defense poked at inconsistencies, exploiting the natural imperfections of memory. The forensics, though stronger than before, remained circumstantial in key areas. Dunlop's lawyers pressed hard on every weak spot, hammering home the message that suspicion was not the same as proof. Once again, the case seemed to drift further away from certainty, leaving jurors with space to question.

Ann sat in the gallery, her emotions swinging between hope and despair. Each piece of testimony in her mind formed a clear and damning picture of Dunlop's guilt. But as she watched the defense dismantle the prosecution's arguments, her optimism wavered. The trial felt less like a search for truth and more like a performance, with Dunlop benefiting from the drama. To Ann, it was unbearable to watch justice slip away for a second time, knowing Julie's story was being twisted into a contest of technicalities.

The verdict was yet another crushing blow. The jury, once again unconvinced, failed to deliver the conviction Ann had so desperately prayed for. Dunlop walked free a second time, emboldened by his victories. For him, it was proof that the law could be bent in his favor, that loopholes and doubt were his shield. For Ann, it was an agony beyond words. She left the courtroom shattered, her grief compounded by the realization that Julie's killer had beaten the system not once, but twice.

What made this collapse even more devastating was the permanence of it. The principle of double jeopardy — a centuries-old safeguard against repeated prosecution — now locked the door on Julie's case. No matter what evidence surfaced, Dunlop could not legally be retried for her murder. The law that was meant to protect the innocent had become a weapon shielding the guilty. For Ann Ming, the trials were over, but her fight for justice had only just begun.

The Double Jeopardy Shield

When the second trial collapsed, Ann Ming was forced to confront a brutal truth: the law was now protecting the man who had taken her daughter's life. The doctrine of double jeopardy, enshrined in British law for more than 800 years, stated that no person could be tried twice for the same crime once acquitted. The principle had been created centuries earlier to prevent the state from persecuting individuals with endless prosecutions, but in Julie Hogg's case, it worked in reverse. Instead of safeguarding the innocent, it gave cover to a guilty man.

For Ann, this was an impossible pill to swallow. She had sat through two trials, endured the re-telling of her daughter's last hours, listened to forensic evidence and seen Dunlop's arrogance on display. Yet, despite the strength of the case, the jury had failed to convict him. And now, the law sealed his freedom, closing the door to any future justice. The very system that was supposed to protect families like hers had instead delivered a devastating betrayal.

In the months after the second trial, Dunlop began to lean on that shield of immunity with brazen confidence. Reports reached Ann that he was bragging in pubs about getting away with the "perfect crime," boasting that the law couldn't touch him no matter what he said. For Ann, every word of these stories was like a knife twisting deeper into her grief. The thought that her daughter's killer was laughing, socializing, and boasting while Julie lay in her grave filled her with both rage and despair.

The weight of the law seemed immovable. Friends and officials told Ann there was nothing more to be done, that the case was closed forever. But she refused to accept that. Her instincts told her that justice should not be bounded by outdated rules when new truths could be brought to light. Each time she thought of Dunlop's smug grin and heard of his boasts, her determination hardened. If the law itself was the barrier, then the law had to change.

At the time, the idea of overturning such an ancient legal principle seemed unimaginable. Judges, lawyers, and politicians all regarded double jeopardy as untouchable. Yet Ann Ming was not intimidated by tradition or authority. She was a mother who had seen the system fail twice, and she would not rest while her daughter's killer walked free. In that moment, what looked to the world like an ending became, for Ann, the beginning of a campaign that would shake the foundations of British justice.

CHAPTER 7: LIVING UNDER THE SHADOW

Dunlop Walks Free

The moment Billy Dunlop walked free from court was one that burned deep into the memory of Julie Hogg's family. Despite two trials and a mountain of circumstantial evidence pointing towards his guilt, the legal system had failed to convict him. For Ann Ming, it felt like a cruel betrayal, not only of her daughter's memory but also of the very idea of justice. She had sat through the court proceedings, heard the testimonies, and watched as jurors wrestled with uncertainty, only for Dunlop to emerge unpunished, his smirk a chilling reminder that he knew the law had granted him protection. To the family, it was as if the courts themselves had conspired to silence the truth.

Dunlop's release sent shockwaves through the community. Many had suspected him from the beginning, and whispers followed him everywhere he went. Yet suspicion could not chain him. He lived openly, drinking in local pubs, sometimes even boasting that he had "got away with murder." These taunts were not confined to back rooms; they were loud, deliberate, and intended to provoke. Each time he flaunted his freedom, it was a cruel twist of the knife in the wounds of Julie's grieving loved ones. The streets of Billingham seemed smaller, darker, overshadowed by the knowledge that a killer could walk among them without consequence.

For Ann Ming, the nightmare only deepened. She could not rest knowing that the man who had strangled her daughter was free, shielded by the law. Each day brought fresh torment as she replayed the trial's failures in her mind—the lack of forensic proof, the jurors' hesitation, the rules that seemed to favor the accused more than the victim. But beyond her private anguish was a burning anger. Ann was not someone who could quietly accept injustice. Her instincts told her that Dunlop's freedom was not the end of the story but the beginning of her fight. She resolved that if the law would not protect her daughter, then she would challenge the very law itself.

Dunlop, emboldened by his acquittals, continued his reckless behavior, convinced he was untouchable. He seemed to revel in the legal loophole that allowed him to walk free. His arrogance, however, only fueled Ann's determination. Each sneer, each boast, each moment he flaunted his freedom added weight to her resolve. Ann refused to let Julie's case become just another unsolved tragedy. She understood the enormity of what lay ahead—taking on centuries-old legal principles, confronting a justice system resistant to change, and waging a battle few believed could be won. But she also knew that silence meant surrender, and surrender was something she could never allow.

The day Dunlop walked free was not the end of the fight; it was the spark that ignited one of the most important legal battles in modern British history. While he may have felt invincible, protected by the double jeopardy rule, Ann Ming was already preparing to prove that no law, no matter how deeply rooted, was beyond challenge. Her daughter's memory deserved nothing less.

The Weight on Ann's Family

The weight of Julie's murder pressed on Ann Ming's family in ways that words could barely capture. Grief, in its rawest form, touched every corner of their lives, making ordinary routines unbearable. Ann would sit at the table, staring at the empty chair where her daughter should have been, while Julie's little boy, Kevin, asked questions too painful to answer. Kevin's innocent face was a constant reminder of what had been stolen, a life torn apart before it had even begun. The family home, once filled with the chatter of children and the warmth of Julie's presence, became a place haunted by silence and aching memories.

Ann carried herself with remarkable strength, but inside, she was unraveling. Nights were the hardest. Sleep eluded her, and when it did come, it was broken by nightmares of Julie's final moments. The image of her daughter hidden behind the bath panel never left her mind. Ann tried to keep the household steady, to shield Kevin and her other children from the storm of grief, but the strain was crushing. Simple joys—holidays, family meals, laughter—felt tainted, as if happiness itself had been stolen from them. Life was now divided into two distinct parts: before Julie's death and after.

Her husband, Charlie, grieved differently. He retreated into silence, struggling to find words for the depth of his sorrow. The weight of watching Ann suffer, knowing he could not take away her pain, made him feel helpless. Their marriage was tested by the strain, but it was also held together by the shared determination to honor their daughter's memory. Each anniversary, each birthday that passed without Julie, was another reminder of all the milestones that had been denied. Family gatherings became bittersweet, with an invisible absence lingering in every celebration.

For Kevin, growing up without his mother was both confusing and cruel. He was too young to fully grasp the enormity of her death but old enough to feel the gap it left. Ann and Charlie tried to be both grandparents and parents, but the hole Julie left in his life could never truly be filled. Watching Kevin grow while knowing Julie would never see him play, laugh, or succeed was another stab of grief that Ann carried daily. Every smile he gave was tinged with the heartbreak that his mother was not there to witness it.

The burden on Ann's family was not just emotional but also societal. The whispers of the community, the media's attention, and the ever-present knowledge that Julie's killer walked free made healing almost impossible. Grief was not something they could carry privately—it was played out in courtrooms, headlines, and gossip. Yet through it all, Ann refused to allow her family to be broken beyond repair. She channeled her sorrow into strength, carrying not only her own grief but also the weight of her family's pain, determined that one day justice would lift at least part of that unbearable load.

CHAPTER 8: A KILLER CONFESSES

The Prison Admission

In the years after his acquittals, Billy Dunlop drifted further into a life of petty crime and violence. He was no longer the focus of investigators for Julie

Hogg's murder, but the shadow of suspicion never left him. For Ann Ming, knowing that the man she believed had killed her daughter was free to live his life while her family carried unbearable grief was a daily torment. What no one could have predicted was that Dunlop's arrogance and recklessness would eventually provide the very crack in the wall that Ann so desperately needed.

While serving time in prison for an unrelated assault, Dunlop began to boast to other inmates about his past. Behind bars, where violence and bravado often spoke louder than truth, he let slip a chilling confession: he had killed Julie Hogg. The admission was not shouted from the rooftops, but rather whispered in that toxic blend of pride and spite. To Dunlop, the double jeopardy law was his shield—he could not be tried again for the same crime, so his words carried no fear of consequence. He flaunted his supposed invincibility, believing the system itself protected him from ever facing true justice.

Word of Dunlop's prison confession eventually reached the authorities, and for Ann, it was like reopening a wound that had never healed. The details confirmed what she had always known in her heart, yet the law remained an immovable barrier. Double jeopardy meant that even with his admission, the courts could not touch him. For a grieving mother, this was not just frustrating—it was intolerable. She could not fathom living in a country where a man could admit to murder and still be protected by outdated legal tradition.

Ann's anger grew into resolve. She refused to accept that her daughter's killer could laugh at the system and remain untouchable. She began documenting Dunlop's admissions, pressing officials, and gathering every scrap of information that could one day force change. The confession was more than just a slip of the tongue—it was a weapon, proof that the law as it stood was broken. Ann understood that if she could not find justice within the system, then she would have to change the system itself.

This prison admission became the turning point, the moment when grief transformed into full-scale activism. For Ann Ming, Dunlop's arrogance was not the end of her fight but the start of a campaign that would shake the foundations of Britain's legal history. It was here, in the darkest corners of a prison cell, that the seeds of justice were unexpectedly planted.

Perjury and Frustration

Billy Dunlop's prison admission was not the only reckless mistake he made. In 1999, he faced a charge of perjury, accused of lying under oath during earlier proceedings connected to Julie Hogg's murder. The case briefly reopened old wounds for Ann Ming, who hoped that at last some form of accountability might emerge. Yet even here, justice seemed to slip away. The perjury charge carried weight, but it was a hollow substitute for the crime everyone knew he had committed. For Ann, it was unbearable to sit in court and hear her daughter's name invoked while the man responsible still evaded the full force of the law.

The frustration of watching Dunlop face only minor consequences was immense. While he was eventually convicted of perjury and served a short prison sentence, it felt like an insult compared to the life he had taken. The legal system seemed more concerned with technicalities than with moral justice. Ann found herself trapped in a nightmare where the law that was meant to protect her family instead became a barrier to truth. Each court appearance reminded her not of progress, but of how far they still had to go.

Ann's anger deepened when Dunlop, smug in his protection under the double jeopardy rule, mocked the very idea of justice. He knew he could not be tried again for Julie's murder, and his behavior reflected a man who believed himself untouchable. For Ann and her family, this arrogance was like salt in an open wound. They were forced to relive their grief while Dunlop played games with the system. It was as though Julie's life had been devalued by the very laws meant to safeguard society.

The perjury case highlighted the absurdity of the situation. Here was a man who had admitted to murder, who had lied in court, and yet who remained shielded from the crime that mattered most. For Ann, it crystallized the truth: the system was broken, and no amount of patience or faith in existing laws would ever deliver justice. The double jeopardy rule, unchallenged for centuries, had become a cruel shield for killers like Dunlop.

This frustration became fuel. Rather than let the injustice crush her spirit, Ann began to channel her energy into change. The perjury trial had shown her that the courts could not, or would not, act on their own. If anything was going to change, it would have to come from outside the courtroom—from her. Ann Ming realized that she could no longer simply fight for her daughter's memory. She would have to fight for the reform of the law itself.

CHAPTER 9: THE CAMPAIGN OF A LIFETIME

Letters, Meetings, and Parliament

Ann Ming's campaign began humbly, with letters written late at night at her kitchen table. She addressed everyone she believed might listen—local MPs, senior police officials, legal experts, and eventually cabinet ministers. Each letter carried not only her grief but also her growing conviction that the law itself had failed. She carefully laid out her case: that Billy Dunlop had confessed to Julie's murder, that he had perjured himself, and that double jeopardy had allowed him to walk free. At first, many replies were polite but dismissive, reminding her that the rule against double jeopardy was centuries old and deeply rooted in British law. Still, Ann kept writing. She refused to allow Julie's memory to be reduced to a file gathering dust.

Her persistence gradually caught the attention of key figures. Ann arranged meetings wherever she could—sometimes in cramped constituency offices, other times in the formal halls of Westminster. She would arrive with her notes, photographs of Julie, and a mother's determination. Facing MPs and ministers, she explained in plain, human terms how absurd it was that a murderer could boast about his crime and remain untouchable. Many of those she spoke to were moved by her sincerity, but some still argued the principle of finality in law outweighed individual cases. Ann countered calmly but firmly, pointing out that principles meant little when they allowed killers to laugh at justice.

The campaign was exhausting. Ann often traveled long distances, sometimes on her own, to make her case. She learned to navigate the bureaucracy of Parliament, to identify allies among politicians, and to apply pressure through the media. Every interview she gave, every article published about her fight, helped bring attention to the issue. What began as one grieving mother's struggle became a cause that ordinary people across Britain could understand. Letters of support began arriving at her home, from strangers who had read about Julie's case and wanted her to know she was not fighting alone.

Inside Parliament, her persistence started to bear fruit. Lawmakers who had once brushed aside her concerns began to discuss the possibility of reform. Ann's meetings with the Home Office grew more serious, and her case was cited in debates about modernizing criminal justice. For Ann, this was a breakthrough: Julie's story was no longer confined to Hartlepool or to her own family's grief. It was shaping national conversations about justice. She had become not only an advocate for her daughter but also the voice for future victims whose killers might exploit the same loophole.

The turning point came when senior figures finally acknowledged that the law could not remain unchanged. The government agreed to review the double jeopardy rule, a prospect that had once seemed impossible. Ann had managed, through sheer determination, to drag an ancient legal principle into the spotlight of modern Britain. The fight was far from over—changing the law would take years, and resistance remained strong—but she had achieved something monumental. By her letters, her meetings, and her unrelenting presence in Parliament, Ann Ming had moved the impossible into the realm of the possible. Julie's memory was no longer only a source of grief—it was the driving force behind a reform that would change British justice forever.

Building Public Support

Ann knew that political pressure alone would not be enough to change a law that had stood for centuries. To succeed, she had to rally the public, to make Julie's story a matter of national concern rather than a private tragedy. She began speaking more openly to the media, giving interviews that highlighted not just her grief but also the injustice at the heart of her daughter's case. Newspapers carried headlines about the "mother fighting the law," and television cameras followed her as she spoke with quiet conviction about why the system had to change. The more the public heard her story, the more outrage grew. People who had never met Julie felt a personal stake in Ann's fight, and they began writing to their MPs, demanding reform.

At community meetings and legal forums, Ann presented her case with the same mix of personal testimony and moral clarity that had begun to sway politicians. She spoke not as a lawyer but as a mother, cutting through legal jargon with plain words that touched hearts. "If a murderer can confess and still escape justice," she would ask, "what protection does that give the rest of us?" Crowds often responded with spontaneous applause, and local journalists wrote moving accounts of her appearances. These moments built momentum, giving her campaign the grassroots energy it needed to grow beyond the walls of Westminster.

Petitions began to circulate, calling for the abolition of the double jeopardy protection in murder cases. Supporters from all walks of life—teachers, police officers, parents, retirees—signed their names, and many sent messages of encouragement to Ann directly. She saved every one, treating them as a reminder that she was not alone in her mission. This groundswell of support provided politicians with evidence that the public wanted change, and it gave Ann leverage in her ongoing meetings with lawmakers. What had once seemed like a lone mother's battle was fast becoming a national movement.

The media, too, played a crucial role in amplifying her voice. Television documentaries revisited Julie's murder, exposing the loophole that allowed Dunlop to remain free despite his admissions. Opinion columns argued that justice should evolve with the times and praised Ann for her persistence. The narrative shifted: this was no longer just the story of a failed prosecution, but a broader test of whether Britain could modernize its legal system to reflect fairness and accountability. Ann's name became synonymous with the push for reform, and Julie's memory became the rallying cry for justice.

By the late 1990s and early 2000s, Ann's campaign had transformed into a powerful moral cause, uniting grieving families, concerned citizens, and sympathetic lawmakers. Every public appearance, every interview, every petition signed added another brick to the foundation of change. Ann had taken her daughter's story beyond the confines of Billingham and made it resonate with the entire country. She had built not only public support but also a sense of urgency that lawmakers could no longer ignore.

CHAPTER 10: OVERTURNING AN ANCIENT LAW

The Criminal Justice Act 2003

The turning point in Ann Ming's relentless campaign came with the passage of the **Criminal Justice Act 2003**, a sweeping piece of legislation that would finally dismantle the ancient shield of double jeopardy in cases of serious crime. After years of setbacks, disappointments, and rejections, Ann's voice had reached the very heart of government. Lawmakers could no longer deny the plain truth she had been shouting into the wind for more than a decade: justice must not end where loopholes begin. For the first time in 800 years, Parliament agreed to reshape one of the cornerstones of English law.

The Act made it possible for retrials to take place if compelling new evidence emerged, particularly in cases of murder, rape, and other grave offenses. It was a legal revolution, balancing the historic need to protect individuals from repeated prosecutions with the public's demand that confessed killers should not walk free on technicalities. Politicians debated fiercely in the House of Commons and the House of Lords, but again and again, Ann's name and Julie's story were invoked as proof of why change was necessary. When the bill was finally passed, supporters recognized it as not just a reform but a rewriting of history—one that would alter the course of justice in Britain forever.

For Ann, the Act represented both victory and validation. She had been told countless times that the law was immovable, that her fight was futile, and that she should let go for the sake of her own health. Yet here it was, written into the statutes of the land, a law that bore her fingerprints on every page. "A little woman from Billingham" had moved Parliament, a phrase she herself often used with quiet pride and disbelief. It was living proof that persistence could bend even the strongest institutions.

The Criminal Justice Act 2003 did not just open the door for Julie's case—it gave hope to countless other families who had endured similar pain. It sent a message to offenders that the law was no longer a safe refuge for lies and confessions spoken in arrogance. For Ann, it also reignited a sense of purpose: now that the law had changed, she could focus on seeing it applied, on ensuring that William Dunlop would finally face the justice he had escaped for so long. Her journey was far from over, but the passage of the Act was the clearest sign yet that the tide had turned in her favor.

With the new law in place, the balance of power shifted dramatically. What once seemed untouchable was now within reach. Prosecutors could revisit Dunlop's case, armed with his own words of admission and the new legal tools at their disposal. For Ann, the Criminal Justice Act was not only a landmark in British legal history but also a personal vindication of every sleepless night, every interview, every march into Westminster's corridors. It was proof that Julie's voice, carried by her mother's will, had changed the law of the land.

How Double Jeopardy Fell

The fall of the double jeopardy rule was not sudden; it was the product of years of grinding effort, frustration, and persistence, with Ann Ming at the center of it all. For centuries, the principle had stood firm: once a person was acquitted, they could never be tried again for the same crime, no matter what evidence surfaced afterward. Legal scholars defended it as essential to protecting citizens from oppressive governments and endless prosecutions. But as Ann's campaign gained momentum, more people began to see the rule not as a safeguard, but as an outdated shield for the guilty. Julie's case became the clearest and most heartbreaking example of why it had to change.

Public pressure, fueled by Ann's tireless advocacy, forced Parliament to examine the issue more seriously. Committees were formed, hearings were held, and voices from across the legal spectrum were invited to weigh in. The arguments were fierce. Critics of reform warned that dismantling double jeopardy could lead to abuses of power, retrials driven by politics rather than justice. But supporters countered with the undeniable facts: new forensic science, like DNA testing, made it possible to uncover truths that earlier juries could never have known. And when a confessed murderer could boast about his crime while remaining legally untouchable, the law had clearly failed.

Ann's presence in these debates was impossible to ignore. She was not a barrister or a politician; she was a grieving mother who spoke with clarity and conviction. Her story cut through centuries of legal tradition and exposed the moral contradiction at the heart of the rule. Each time she sat before a committee or gave a press interview, she asked the same unanswerable question: how could justice mean protecting a man who had admitted to killing her daughter? Over time, her voice joined with others—journalists, campaigners, victims' families—until the call for reform became a chorus that Parliament could not silence.

When the Criminal Justice Act 2003 was passed, it marked the official collapse of the rule as it had once existed. Murderers and serious offenders could now face retrial if new and compelling evidence came to light. For many, it was almost unthinkable: the undoing of an 800-year-old tradition that had shaped English law since the Middle Ages. But for Ann, it was justice catching up with common sense. The law had finally bent to the reality of modern crime and the needs of modern victims.

The fall of double jeopardy was not just a legal milestone; it was a human victory. It proved that the persistence of one determined woman could achieve what generations of lawyers and politicians had never dared to attempt. And while Ann took pride in knowing that her struggle had helped reshape the law for countless families, her focus remained the same: making sure William Dunlop finally faced the justice he had so long evaded.

CHAPTER 11: JUSTICE AT THE OLD BAILEY

Dunlop Retrial and Conviction

When the Criminal Justice Act 2003 finally came into force, it opened the door to the one outcome Ann Ming had fought for over thirteen long years: the chance to see William Dunlop back in the dock. The Crown Prosecution Service moved swiftly, aware that this was not only a legal test of the new law but also a moment of enormous public interest. Dunlop's prison confessions, once useless in the shadow of double jeopardy, were now the cornerstone of a fresh prosecution. For Ann, hearing that a retrial had been authorized was both overwhelming and surreal. The system that had failed her so many times was finally offering her the chance at justice.

The retrial took place at the Old Bailey in 2006, one of the most famous criminal courts in the world. The weight of history seemed to hang in the air as prosecutors laid out the case. They reminded the jury not only of the original evidence but also of Dunlop's own words, in which he had confessed to killing Julie. This time, there was no loophole to shield him. The defense tried to argue that his confessions were unreliable, the ramblings of a man trying to gain attention or sympathy while behind bars. But the jury could see the truth plainly: Dunlop had admitted the crime, and his guilt could no longer be hidden behind technicalities.

Ann sat through the proceedings, just as she had during the earlier trials, but this time with a different kind of strength. She was no longer just a grieving mother fighting for her daughter; she was a campaigner whose work had helped rewrite British law. Still, the emotions were raw. Hearing once again the details of Julie's murder tore at her heart, but she endured it because she knew what was at stake. Each day in court brought her closer to the justice she had been denied for so long.

When the jury returned with a guilty verdict, the weight of thirteen years seemed to lift. Dunlop was sentenced to life imprisonment, finally held accountable for the crime he had so arrogantly admitted. Ann wept openly in court, surrounded by family members who had shared in her long struggle. The victory was bittersweet—nothing could bring Julie back—but the knowledge that her killer would never walk free again was a measure of peace. For Ann, it was the culmination of years of persistence, sacrifice, and courage.

The conviction was more than justice for Julie; it was proof that change was possible. The new law had worked as intended, delivering accountability where once there had been only despair. For Ann, the moment was deeply personal, but it also belonged to every victim's family who had ever felt abandoned by the system. Dunlop's conviction stood as both a conclusion to her battle and a testament to the power of one mother's unyielding fight for truth.

A Mother's Victory After 17 Years

Seventeen years after Julie Hogg's murder, Ann Ming finally stood on the other side of the battle she had waged with unrelenting determination. The conviction of Billy Dunlop was not simply a legal outcome; it was a personal victory that had demanded every ounce of her strength, courage, and persistence. For nearly two decades, Ann had lived in a cycle of grief and struggle, fighting against institutions that told her again and again that nothing could be done. Yet she had refused to accept the impossible. When the guilty verdict was finally read in 2006, it marked the end of a long road where she had transformed from a grieving mother into a figure who reshaped the very foundations of British justice.

The victory was deeply emotional. Ann's tears in court were not just for Julie, but for the years of frustration, exhaustion, and despair she had carried in silence. She had faced indifference from authorities, endured whispers that she should "move on," and seen her family strain under the weight of her relentless campaign. But that moment in court, watching Dunlop receive a life sentence, was her answer to everyone who doubted her resolve. She had promised Julie she would never stop fighting, and she had kept that promise, even when the odds seemed insurmountable.

This triumph also carried a symbolic weight beyond the courtroom. Ann's persistence had directly led to the fall of an 800-year-old legal shield. By challenging double jeopardy, she had paved the way for countless other families to see justice served when new evidence emerged. Her campaign was not just for Julie; it was for every victim who had been silenced by outdated laws. The Criminal Justice Act 2003 and Dunlop's conviction stood as living proof that ordinary people could bring about extraordinary change. Ann's personal victory became a national one, reshaping the legal landscape in Britain forever.

Even in victory, however, Ann never lost sight of what she had lost. Julie's absence remained a constant shadow, a reminder that no legal triumph could heal the wound left by her murder. Ann often said she would have traded every award, every recognition, for just one more day with her daughter. Yet she also recognized that Julie's legacy lived on—not only through her son Kevin but also in the laws that bore her story. The fight had been grueling, but it had ensured that Julie's name would be remembered not as a statistic, but as the catalyst for change.

By the time Dunlop was locked away for life, Ann had become a symbol of resilience. She showed that the voice of one mother could reverberate through the highest halls of power, forcing change in places where reform had long been resisted. Her victory after seventeen years was not just about holding a killer accountable, but about proving that justice, however delayed, could still be won. Ann had turned unbearable grief into unstoppable resolve, and in doing so, she secured both justice for her daughter and hope for families yet to come.

CHAPTER 12: LEGACY AND REFLECTION

Ann Ming's Recognition and MBE

Ann Ming's tireless fight for justice did not go unnoticed. After years of battling in courts, pressing lawmakers, and turning her grief into a national cause, her efforts were formally recognized when she was awarded an MBE (Member of the Order of the British Empire). The honor, bestowed for her services to justice, symbolized not just her personal triumph but also the acknowledgment by the nation that one woman's determination had reshaped British law. It was an emotional moment, both for Ann and for those who had stood beside her through the long, painful journey. The award was not just a medal—it was a seal of validation that her relentless pursuit of truth had changed the course of history.

For Ann, the MBE represented far more than ceremonial recognition. It stood as proof that the countless nights of grief, the frustration at collapsed trials, the despair of watching Dunlop walk free, and the exhaustion of lobbying politicians had all been worth it. She had been told repeatedly that nothing could be done, that the law was unmovable, that justice for Julie was out of reach. Yet she had refused to accept those answers. By receiving such an honor, Ann demonstrated to other grieving families that persistence and courage could indeed move mountains, even when the system seemed immovable.

The ceremony itself carried a deeply personal weight. While Ann accepted the MBE with pride, her thoughts inevitably returned to Julie. It was her daughter's memory that had fueled every step of her campaign, and the medal was a bittersweet reminder of why the battle had begun. In every speech and every public appearance, Ann made sure Julie's name remained at the heart of the story. The award, therefore, was not just for Ann, but for Julie too—for the life that had been cut short, and for the justice that had been so long denied.

Beyond personal pride, Ann's recognition also had broader implications. It signaled a cultural shift in how victims' families were perceived and treated within the justice system. By honoring Ann, the establishment was effectively admitting that the law had failed her family, and that her intervention had been necessary to correct that failure. It was a rare acknowledgment that sometimes the greatest reforms come not from inside institutions, but from ordinary people demanding change from the outside. Ann's MBE embodied this truth, highlighting her role not just as a grieving mother, but as a reformer who had made Britain more just.

For Ann and her family, the MBE was both a conclusion and a new beginning. While nothing could ever bring Julie back, the recognition meant her death had not been in vain. The change in the law and Dunlop's eventual conviction were part of Julie's legacy, a testament to her mother's devotion. Ann's recognition ensured that her story would not fade into obscurity but would continue to inspire others—both those fighting personal battles and those striving for systemic change. It was the final proof that even in the darkest circumstances, resilience, love, and determination could carve a path to justice.

How Her Fight Changed Britain

Ann Ming's fight did more than bring justice for Julie—it reshaped the very foundations of British law. Before her campaign, the centuries-old principle of double jeopardy was seen as untouchable, a safeguard that ensured no one could be tried twice for the same crime. While it was designed to protect the innocent from persecution, in practice it sometimes shielded the guilty. Julie's case exposed this flaw in the starkest terms, forcing the nation to confront the reality that the law, while meant to uphold justice, had in fact obstructed it. Ann's relentless challenge to that principle became the catalyst for one of the most significant legal reforms in modern Britain.

Her campaign revealed that justice systems cannot remain static; they must evolve alongside advances in science and the demands of fairness. DNA technology and new forensic methods meant evidence could surface years after a trial, yet under the old rules, such breakthroughs were useless if a verdict had already been delivered. Ann made sure that policymakers, judges, and the public understood this contradiction. By pressing Parliament, writing letters, and speaking to the media, she transformed a personal tragedy into a national conversation about justice, rights, and responsibility.

The eventual reform—the Criminal Justice Act 2003—allowed for retrials in serious cases where compelling new evidence emerged. This landmark change directly addressed the kind of miscarriage of justice that Ann and her family had endured. It was no small shift; it overturned a legal principle that had stood for over 800 years. Critics argued it weakened protections for defendants, but supporters pointed out that it balanced those rights against the rights of victims and society as a whole. Without Ann Ming's persistence, this balance might never have been struck, and countless other families would have faced the same heartbreak she had.

Her fight also changed how ordinary people saw their own power in shaping the law. Ann was not a lawyer, politician, or public figure when her battle began—she was a grieving mother from Teesside. Yet her voice carried far beyond her community, proving that determination, moral clarity, and persistence could succeed where institutions had failed. She became a symbol of resilience, showing that even the most entrenched laws could be re-examined and reformed if justice demanded it.

Ultimately, Ann Ming's fight created a legacy that extends beyond her own family's tragedy. By ensuring that the guilty could no longer hide behind outdated protections, she made Britain a fairer, more accountable place. Her work continues to echo in courtrooms, where new trials proceed under rules that exist because of her. Julie's memory is preserved not only in the love of her family, but in a legal system that now better serves victims and the truth. Ann's story is a testament to how one voice, guided by love and unwavering conviction, can change an entire nation.

CONCLUSION

The story of Ann Ming is not only the story of a mother's love but also a story of justice wrestled from the grip of failure. For seventeen long years, she lived with the unbearable weight of knowing her daughter's killer was free, while the law itself stood as a barrier to the truth. Yet in that darkness, Ann refused to give in. She fought with courage, resilience, and an unshakable belief that justice, however delayed, was still worth pursuing.

Julie Hogg's life was cut tragically short, but through Ann's fight, her memory became the driving force behind a reform that changed Britain forever. The battles in courtrooms, the endless letters to officials, the countless meetings with politicians—each step carved a path toward a justice system that could no longer allow the guilty to hide behind technicalities. Ann's struggle showed that even the most ancient laws are not beyond question when they stand in the way of what is right.

In the end, the conviction of Billy Dunlop was more than a personal victory; it was a victory for truth, for fairness, and for every family who might one day walk a similar path. Ann's determination ensured that future victims and their families would not have to endure the same torment she did. She turned heartbreak into action, and action into lasting change.

This is the legacy of Ann Ming: a mother who refused silence, a woman who reshaped the law of a nation, and a voice that continues to inspire all who believe that justice must prevail. Her story is proof that perseverance can overcome even the strongest barriers, and that love, sharpened by grief, can move mountains. Julie's memory lives on not only in the hearts of her family, but also in the laws of Britain—a reminder that one life, though lost too soon, can still change the world.

Printed in Dunstable, United Kingdom